THE OPEN MEDIA PAMPHLET SERIES

THE OPEN MEDIA PAMPHLET SERIES

Corporate Media and the Threat to Democracy

ROBERT W. McCHESNEY

SEVEN STORIES PRESS / New York

A Seven Stories Press First Edition,
published in association with Open Media.

Open Media Pamphlet Series editors,
Greg Ruggiero and Stuart Sahulka.

Library of Congress Cataloging-in-Publication Data

McChesney, Robert W.
    Corporate Media and the Threat to Democracy /
        by Robert W. McChesney.
    p.   cm. —(The Open Media Pamphlet Series)
    ISBN 1-888363-47-9
    1. Communication, International. 2. Mass media—
Economic aspects. 3. Communication—International
cooperation. 4. Democracy. I. Title. II. Series.
P96.I5M337 1997
302.2—dc21   96-37525
                                              CIP

Book design by Cindy LaBreacht

9 8 7 6 5 4 3 2 1

Participatory self-government, or democracy, works best when at least three criteria are met. First, it helps when there are not significant disparities in economic wealth and property ownership across the society. Such disparities undermine the ability of citizens to act as equals. Second, it helps when there is a sense of community and a notion that an individual's well-being is determined to no small extent by the community's well-being. This provides democratic political culture with a substance that cannot exist if everyone is simply out to advance narrowly defined self-interests, even if those interests might be harmful to the community as a whole. Third, democracy requires that there be an effective system of political communication, broadly construed, that informs and engages the citizenry, drawing people meaningfully into the polity. This becomes especially important as societies grow larger and more complex, but has been true for all societies dedicated toward self-government. While democracies by definition must respect individual freedoms, these freedoms can only be exercised in a meaningful sense when the citizenry is informed, engaged, and participating. Moreover, without this, political debate can scarcely address the central issues of power and resource allocation that must be at the heart of public deliberation in a democracy. As James Madison noted, "A popular government without popular information, or the means of acquiring it, is but a prologue to a farce or a tragedy, or perhaps both."[1]

These three criteria are related. In non-democratic societies those in power invariably dominate the communication systems to maintain their rule. In democratic societies the manner by which the media system is structured, controlled and subsidized is of central political importance. Control over the means of communication is an integral aspect of political and economic power. In many nations, to their credit, media policy debates have been and are important political issues. In the United States, to the contrary, private commercial control over communication is often regarded as innately democratic and benevolent, and therefore not subject to political discussion. Government involvement with media or communication is almost universally denigrated in the U.S. as a direct invitation to tyranny, no matter how well intended. The preponderance of U.S. mass communication is controlled by less than two dozen enormous profit-maximizing corporations, which receive much of their income from advertising placed largely by other huge

ROBERT W. McCHESNEY

corporations. But the extent of this media ownership and control goes generally unremarked in the media and intellectual culture, and there appears to be little sense of concern about its dimensions among the citizenry as a whole.

In my view, private control over media and communication is not a neutral or necessarily a benevolent proposition. The commercial basis of U.S. media has negative implications for the exercise of political democracy: it encourages a weak political culture that makes depoliticization, apathy and selfishness rational choices for the citizenry, and it permits the business and commercial interests that actually rule U.S. society to have inordinate influence over media content. In short, the nature of the U.S. media system undermines all three of the meaningful criteria necessary for self-government. Accordingly, for those committed to democracy, it is imperative to reform the media system. This is not going to be an easy task, for there is no small amount of confusion over what would be a superior democratic alternative to the status quo. The political obstacles seem even more daunting because the terrain is no longer local or even national. Media politics are becoming global in scope, as the commercial media market assumes global proportions and as it is closely linked to the globalizing market economy. The immensity of the task of changing and democratizing media is sobering, but it is a job that must be done.

Media corporations also make unusually powerful adversaries for proponents of media reform. They not only enjoy significant political and economic power, but, of course, they also control the media that must provide much of the information citizens need to evaluate media conduct. Moreover, the corporate media system is also protected by several powerful myths, that in combination make it nearly impossible to broach the subject of media reform in U.S. political culture. These myths include: that an advertising-supported, profit-driven media system was ordained by the Founding Fathers and the First Amendment; that professionalism in journalism will protect the public interest from private media control; that the Internet and new digital technologies with their billions of potential channels eliminate any reason to be concerned about corporate domination of media; that the market is the best possible organization for a media system because it forces media firms to "give the people what they want"; that a commercial media system was selected historically in public debate as the best possible system for a democracy, and the matter has therefore been determined for all time; and that the media are not dominated by corporate interests but, instead, have a liberal or left-wing anti-business bias.

The first task for changing the media system is to put control of the media on the political agenda—exactly where it belongs in a democratic society. The purpose of this essay is to assist in that process, by providing an analysis of the contours and trajectory of the contemporary media system. In particular, I sketch out ownership and subsidy patterns of the commercial media system and argue that these present a direct threat to the ability of the United States to have a viable democratic media culture. I also debunk—or at least qualify—the ideological myths that shield corporate control of the media from public scrutiny. I con-

ROBERT W. McCHESNEY

clude by specifically discussing what is being done and what needs to be done to construct a democratic media.

THE PROBLEM OF JOURNALISM

Media systems provide many types of content, including numerous varieties of entertainment and journalism. Although entertainment and cultural fare can and do provide vital social and political commentary and information, this is a direct responsibility of journalism. A healthy political culture requires that to some extent each of these forms of communication be politicized—open to public questioning and discussion. In the absence of a viable democratic journalism, art and entertainment may fill some of the breach, but they will likely accommodate themselves to the depoliticized or repressive political culture. Indeed, the burden upon journalism to provide political information is increased in the modern media marketplace, where commercial values tend to discourage the "politicization" of entertainment and cultural material beyond a fairly narrow and safe range.

How best to provide a democratic journalism, broadly construed to include public affairs as well as "news," is a difficult problem for any democracy. To the extent that journalism deals with politics, it will always be a source of some controversy. Moreover, journalism requires institutional support and subsidy of some kind, and it reflects the conscious decisions of editors and reporters, not to mention those that hire and fire them. In short, journalism can never be an entirely neutral enterprise. And, if one de-emphasizes the goal of neutrality, attempting to make it accurately reflect the range of perspectives in a society, especially in an inegalitarian society, is no easy task. With this in mind, and in view of the complex nature of modern societies, it seems likely that there is no one "solution" to the problem of journalism.

In recent years the work of Jurgen Habermas and others has pointed toward a way of conceptualizing a democratic media.[2] According to Habermas, a critical factor that led to the rise and success of democratic revolutions and societies in the 18th and 19th centuries was the emergence—for the first time in modern history—of a "public sphere" for democratic discourse. This public sphere was a "space" independent of both state and business control which permitted citizens to interact, study and debate on the public issues of the day without fear of immediate reprisal from the political and economic powers that be. The media existed in the public sphere, but they were only part of it.

Although Habermas's model is idealized, the notion of the public sphere provides a useful framework for democratic media activists. In Habermas's view, the public sphere loses its democratic capacities as it is taken over by either the state or business or some combination of the two. In the United States, clearly, business and commercial values have come to dominate the media as perhaps nowhere else in the world. To reassert the "public sphere" notion of a media system would require a major commitment to nonprofit and noncommercial media, at the very least, and perhaps a good deal else. But the public sphere framework only points in the direction of solutions; there are probably any number of workable alternatives. The immediate objective for media

ROBERT W. McCHESNEY

activists is to get this long neglected subject on the political agenda and to encourage public participation.

Even if the "public sphere" is based on an idealized interpretation of western media history, it contradicts the prevailing mythology of a "free press," which is widely cherished in the United States. Indeed, the power of the corporate media rests to no small extent upon the myth that only a commercial capitalist media system that produces "unbiased" journalism can be truly democratic, and that this was the express purpose of the Founding Fathers as they crafted the First Amendment to the U.S. Constitution. In fact, U.S. history reveals a media culture that is unrecognizable by the standards of the myth. The Founding Fathers, to the extent we can generalize, envisioned a press that above all else would stimulate public involvement—what media historian John Nerone has termed the "town meeting" metaphor of the press. In the first 50 or 60 years of the republic, journalism moved away from that ideal and became highly partisan. It was not especially profitable and was often subsidized directly or indirectly by government printing contracts, political parties or factions. Advertising played a minor and unimportant role, and did not exist in the modern sense of the term. The press was closely linked to the political culture of the day; any given city might have several newspapers providing very different interpretations of public issues. Some modern scholars term this era the "Dark Ages of American Journalism," the assumption being that these partisan newspapers operated as propaganda sheets, not unlike the Stalinist or Nazi media. The key ingredient of Nazi and Stalinist journals was that opposing viewpoints were banned. In a democratic system, where differing perspectives are protected by the constitution, a diverse partisan press tends to produce a highly informed and engaged citizenry. Hence the Jacksonian era (1820s and 1830s), the last great period of partisan journalism, is sometimes characterized as the "Golden Age of American Politics," for its high level of political interest and participation.

All of this began to change around the 1840s when entrepreneurs began to realize that they could make lots of money publishing newspapers. By the end of the Civil War, the partisan system had been displaced by a dynamic and vibrant commercial newspaper system. "America is the classic soil of newspapers; everybody is reading," an English writer observed in 1871. "No political party, or religious sect, no theological school, no literary or benevolent association, is without its particular organ; there is a universality of print."[3] Throughout the balance of the 19th century, the newspaper industry was highly competitive. Many newspapers served every major market. Newspapers developed enormous circulations and penetrated every niche of society. The press tended to remain partisan by contemporary standards, but its fundamental reason for being was now profit, not political influence, and this contributed to fundamentally altering the way editors, publishers, and, eventually, the public thought about journalism.[4]

Two critical developments crystallized by the beginning of the 20th century, just when the political economy was becoming dominated by large corporations. First, newspapers grew bigger and bigger and

ROBERT W. McCHESNEY

their markets grew increasingly concentrated. The largest newspaper in a market might now reach 40 to 60 percent of the population, rather than 10 percent, as had been the case in 1875. Second, with the rise of corporate capitalism, advertising emerged as the dominant source of income for the press. This had enormous consequences. Most advertisers sought out newspapers with the highest circulations, which drove most other papers in a market out of business. In this context, highly partisan journalism tended to be bad business. Wanting the largest possible circulation to dangle before advertisers, publishers did not want to upset any significant part of their potential readership. Moreover, as the control of newspapers in each market became concentrated among one or two or three owners, and as ownership concentrated nationally in the form of chains, journalism came to reflect the partisan interests of owners and advertisers, rather than diverse interests in any given community.

This was the context for the emergence of professional journalism schools, which were nonexistent at the turn of the century but were training a significant percentage of the nation's reporters by 1920. The core idea behind professional journalism was that news should not be influenced by the political agendas of the owners and advertisers, or by the editors and journalists themselves. At its crudest, this doctrine is characterized as "objectivity," whereby trained professionals develop "neutral" news values so that accounts of public affairs are the same regardless of who the reporter is, or which medium carries the report. Professional journalism's mission was to make a capitalist, advertising-supported media system seem—at least superficially—to be an objective source of news to many citizens.

The newly emergent professional journalism was a very different animal from its partisan ancestor. It was hardly neutral. On one hand, the commercial requirements for media content to satisfy media owners and advertisers were built implicitly into the professional ideology; were that not the case, owners and advertisers would have been far more hostile to the rise of professional journalism than they were. On the other hand, corporate activities and the affairs of the wealthy were not subject to the same degree of scrutiny as government practices; the professional codes deemed the affairs of powerful economic actors vastly less newsworthy than the activities of politicians. In this manner "objective" journalism effectively internalized corporate capitalism as the natural order for a democracy. Thus, as Ben Bagdikian puts it, journalists became oblivious to the compromises with authority they constantly make.[5]

Moreover, in its pursuit of "objectivity," professional journalism proved a lifeless enterprise. In order to avoid the controversy associated with determining which news stories to emphasize and which to de-emphasize, it came to accept official sources (government, big business) as appropriate generators of legitimate news. It also looked for news "events" or "hooks" to justify story selection. This gave the news a very "establishment" orientation, since anything government officials or prominent business people said was seen as newsworthy by definition. It was a safe course of action for journalists and a fairly inexpensive way for publishers to fill the news hole. This practice

14   ROBERT W. McCHESNEY

was soon exploited by politicians and public figures, who learned how to take advantage of their roles as legitimate news sources by carefully manipulating their coverage. More importantly, the emergence of professional journalism was quickly followed by the establishment of public relations as an industry whose primary function it was to generate favorable coverage in the press without public awareness of its activities. By many surveys, press releases and PR-generated material today account for between 40 and 70 percent of the news in today's media.[6]

The new professional journalism is of course not solely responsible for the depoliticization of American society. This is a broad, complex historical phenomenon with many factors. It is worth noting that, as the market expands its influence and commercialism undermines and replaces the role of traditional non-profit organizations in bringing people and communities together, the "public sphere" where individuals become citizens is reduced and corrupted.[7] Moreover, the rise of corporate-dominated capitalism in the 20th century has seen a shift such that core political decisions concerning resource allocation and affairs of state tend to be made by elites outside of public purview, and the political culture concentrates upon tangential or symbolic issues.[8] The range of debate between the dominant U.S. parties tends to closely resemble the range of debate within the business class. This is a context that makes depoliticization a rational choice for much of the citizenry, especially the dispossessed whose fate appears to be affected only marginally by changes in power. "Free market" conservatives like Milton Friedman are unapologetic about this turn of events; in their view the market (i.e. business) should rule and the political system should logically deal with how best to protect private property and not much else. It is counterproductive for citizens to apply much attention or energy to public life, except to chastise those who criticize business.[9] As Noam Chomsky has observed, when traditionally apathetic sectors of the population became politically active and demanded a say in basic political issues in the 1960s and 1970s, elite business and intellectual figures characterized this as a "crisis of democracy," and with no sense of irony.[10]

Yet no institution is more important to the public sphere than the media, so as journalism became "professionalized" it played a major role in assisting the depoliticization of U.S. society. By defining the news as being based on specific events or on the activities of official sources, the news media neglect coverage of long-term social issues that dominate society. Moreover, by sanitizing coverage and seemingly depriving it of ideological content, the news made public affairs increasingly obtuse, confusing and boring. The excitement once associated with politics was now to be found only in coverage of crime, sports and celebrities. This depoliticization has been marked by a general decline in political knowledge, by lower voter turnouts, and by a narrowing range of legitimate political debate.

To be sure, professionalism did bring a certain degree of autonomy to the newsroom and permit journalists to pursue stories with far more freedom than would have been the case in the 19th century. On certain types of issues that clear the professional criteria for selection, commercial journalism has been and is first-rate. Moreover, there have been countless outstanding U.S. journalists throughout the 20th century—and there still are—thoroughly committed to the democratic and progressive aspects of the professional journalistic ideology. Even so, the dominant institutional factors have pressed for a decontextualized, depoliticized and conservative journalism. By the early 1980s, these characteristics had been observed and chronicled widely by numerous scholars including Gaye Tuchman, Herbert Gans, Mark Fishman, and W. Lance Bennett.[11] Edward S. Herman and Noam Chomsky have demonstrated how, on the fundamental political issues of the day, journalism tends to conform to elite interests, and to avoid antagonizing the powers-that-be.[12] Indeed, in what stands as perhaps the most damning statement one could make about the news media, some studies have suggested that the more a person consumes commercial news, the less capable that person is of understanding politics or public affairs.[13]

CORPORATE MEDIA CONSOLIDATION

The journalism that emerged in the 20th century is a product well suited to the needs of the dominant media firms and advertisers that profited from the status quo. Yet the system was far from stable. On the one hand, new technologies like radio and television emerged and changed many aspects of media and journalism. On the other hand, the market moved inexorably toward becoming an integrated oligopoly, with a handful of firms dominating all forms of U.S. media, from radio, television, music and film to newspapers, magazines, and book publishing. In the early 1980s, Ben Bagdikian's *The Media Monopoly* concluded that less than 50 firms had come to dominate the entirety of the U.S. media, with the result that journalism was increasingly losing its ability to address the role and nature of corporate power in the U.S. political economy. As Bagdikian put it, the range of debate in U.S. journalism concerning capitalism and corporate power was roughly equivalent to the range of debate in the Soviet media concerning the nature of communism and the activities of the Communist Party. In the decade following the publication of *The Media Monopoly*, as traditional ownership regulations were relaxed, the market continued to consolidate at an even faster rate. By the time of the fourth edition of The Media Monopoly, in 1992, Bagdikian calculated that mergers and acquisitions had reduced the number of dominant media firms to two dozen.

Since 1992 there has been an unprecedented wave of mergers and acquisitions among media giants, highlighted by the Time Warner purchase of Turner and the Disney acquisition of Cap Cities/ABC. Fewer than ten colossal vertically integrated media conglomerates now dominate U.S. media. The five largest firms—with annual sales in the $10-25 billion range—are News Corporation, Time Warner, Disney, Viacom, and TCI. These firms are major producers of entertainment and media software and have distribution networks like television networks, cable channels and retail stores. Time Warner, for example, owns music recording studios, film and television production studios, several cable television channels, cable broadcasting systems, amusement parks, the WB television network, book publishing houses, magazine publishing interests,

ROBERT W. McCHESNEY

retail stores, motion picture theaters, and much else. In most of the above categories, Time Warner ranks among the top five firms in the world. The next three media firms include NBC (owned by General Electric), Universal (formerly MCA, owned by Seagram), and Sony. All three of these firms are conglomerates with non-media interests, with Sony and GE being huge electronics concerns that at least double the annual sales of any other media firm.

Below this first group there are another dozen or so quite large media firms—usually conglomerates—with annual sales generally in the $2-5 billion range.[14] This list includes Westinghouse (owner of CBS), Gannett, Cox Enterprises, The New York Times, Advance Communications, Comcast, Hearst, Tribune Co., The Washington Post Co., Knight-Ridder, Times-Mirror, DirecTV (owned by General Motors and AT&T), Dow Jones, Reader's Digest, and McGraw-Hill. By the year 2000 it is probable that some of these firms will make deals to get larger or be acquired by other firms seeking to get larger.

The most striking development in the 1990s has been the emergence of a global commercial media market, utilizing new technologies and the global trend toward de-regulation. A global oligopolistic market that covers the spectrum of media is now crystallizing with very high barriers to entry. National markets remain, and they are indispensable for understanding any particular national situation, but they are becoming secondary in importance. The U.S. based firms just named dominate the global media market along with a handful of European-based firms and a few Latin American and Asian operations. By all accounts they will do so for a long time to come.[15] Firms like Disney and Time Warner have seen their non-U.S. revenues climb from around 15 percent in 1990 to 30 percent in 1996. Sometime in the next decade both firms expect to earn a majority of their income outside of the United States. What stimulates much of the creation of a global media market is the growth in commercial advertising worldwide, especially by transnational firms. Advertising tends to be conducted by large firms operating in oligopolistic markets. With the increasing globalization of the world economy, advertising has come to play a crucial role for the few hundred firms that dominate it. From this vantage point it becomes clear, also, how closely linked the U.S. and global media systems are to the market economy.[16]

Media firms have great incentive to merge, acquire, and globalize. It is when the effects of sheer size, conglomeration, and globalization are combined that a sense of the profit potential emerges. When Disney produces a film, for example, it can also guarantee the film showings on pay cable television and commercial network television, it can produce and sell soundtracks based on the film, it can create spin-off television series, it can produce related amusement park rides, CD-roms, books, comics, and merchandise to be sold in Disney retail stores. Moreover, Disney can promote the film and related material incessantly across all its media properties. In this climate, even films that do poorly at the box office can become profitable. Disney's *Hunchback of Notre Dame* (1996) generated a disappointing $99 million at the North American box office.

ROBERT W. McCHESNEY

However, according to *Adweek* magazine, it is expected to generate $500 million in profit (not just revenues), after the other revenue streams are taken into account. And films that are hits can become spectacularly successful. Disney's *The Lion King* (1994) earned several hundred million at the box office, yet generated over $1 billion in profit for Disney.[17] Moreover, media conglomerates can and do use the full force of their various media holdings to promote their other holdings. They do so incessantly. In sum, the profit whole for the vertically integrated firm can be significantly greater than the profit potential of the individual parts in isolation. Firms without this cross-selling and cross-promotional potential are simply incapable of competing in the global marketplace.

In establishing new ventures, media firms are likely to participate in joint ventures, whereby they link up—usually through shared ownership—with one or more other media firms on specific media projects. Joint ventures are attractive because they reduce the capital requirements and risk on individual firms and permit the firms to spread their resources more widely. Each of the eight largest U.S. media firms has, on average, joint ventures with four of the other seven giants. They each also have even more ventures with smaller media firms. Beyond joint ventures, there is also overlapping direct ownership of these firms. Seagram, owner of MCA, for example, owns 15 percent of Time Warner and has other media equity holdings.[18] TCI is a major shareholder in Time Warner and has holdings in numerous other media firms.[19] The Capital Group Companies mutual fund, valued at $250 billion, is among the very largest shareholders in TCI, News Corporation, Seagram, Time Warner, Viacom, Disney, Westinghouse, and several other smaller media firms.[20]

Even without joint ventures and cross-ownership, competition in oligopolistic media markets is hardly "competitive" in the economic sense of the term. Reigning oligopolistic markets are dominated by a handful of firms that compete—often quite ferociously within the oligopolistic framework—on a non-price basis and are protected by severe barriers to entry. The "synergies" of recent mergers rest on and enhance monopoly power. No start-up studio, for example, has successfully joined the Hollywood oligopoly in 60 years.[21] Rupert Murdoch of News Corporation poses the rational issue for an oligopolistic firm when pondering how to proceed in the media market: "We can join forces now, or we can kill each other and then join forces."[22]

When one lays the map of joint ventures over the global media marketplace, even the traditional levels of competition associated with oligopolistic markets may be exaggerated. "Nobody can really afford to get mad with their competitors," says TCI chairman John Malone, "because they are partners in one area and competitors in another."[23] *The Wall Street Journal* observes that media "competitors wind up switching between the roles of adversaries, prized customers and key partners."[24] In this sense the U.S. and global media and communication market exhibits tendencies not only of an oligopoly, but of a cartel or at least a "gentleman's club."

CORPORATE MEDIA CULTURE

The corporate media produce some excellent fare, and much that is good, especially in the production of entertainment material in commercially lucrative genres. But in view of the extraordinary resources the corporate media command, the quality is woeful. In the final analysis, this is a thoroughly commercial system with severe limitations for our politics and culture. As George Gerbner puts it, the media giants "have nothing to tell, but plenty to sell." The corporate media are carpet-bombing people with advertising and commercialism, whether they like it or not. Moreover, the present course is one where much of the world's entertainment and journalism will be provided by a handful of enormous firms, with invariably pro-profit and pro-global market political positions on the central issues of our times. The implications for political democracy, by any standard, are troubling.

One need only look at the United States to see where and how journalism factors into the operations of the media giants. By the end of the 1980s, the wheels had come off U.S. journalism. In the new world of conglomerate capitalism the goal of the entire media product was to have a direct positive effect on the firm's earnings statement. The press, and the broadcast media, too, increasingly use surveys to locate the news that would be enjoyed by the affluent market desired by advertisers.[25] This, in itself, seriously compromises a major tenet of journalism: that the news should be determined by the public interest, not by the self-interest of owners or advertisers. It also meant that media firms effectively wrote off the bottom 15-50 percent of U.S. society, depending upon the medium. As newspapers, for example, have become increasingly dependent upon advertising revenues for support, they have become anti-democratic forces in society. When newspapers still received primary support from circulation income, they courted every citizen with the funds necessary to purchase the paper, often a pittance. But now they are reliant on advertisers whose sole concern is access to targeted markets. Hence media managers aggressively court the affluent while the balance of the population is pushed to the side. Indeed, the best journalism being done today is that directed to the business class by *The Wall Street Journal*, *Business Week*, and the like. We have quality journalism aimed at the affluent and directed to their needs and interests, and schlock journalism for the masses. As Walter Cronkite observes, intense commercial pressures have converted television journalism into "a stew of trivia, soft features and similar tripe."[26]

To do effective journalism is expensive, and corporate managers realize that the surest way to fatten profits is to fire editors and reporters and fill the news hole with inexpensive syndicated material and fluff. The result has been a sharp polarization among journalists, with salaries and benefits climbing for celebrity and privileged journalists at the elite news media while conditions have deteriorated for the balance of the working press. Layoffs among news workers have been widespread in the past decade; one study reveals that there has been a marked decrease in the number of Washington network correspondents alone in that period.[27] With all this unemployment, salaries for non-elite journalists have plummeted, and beginning salaries are so low that young journalists have a difficult time supporting themselves. These developments have contributed to a collapse in the morale of U.S journalists, a real loss of faith in their enterprise.

The past few years have seen several major editors and journalists leave the profession in anger over these trends.[28] James Squires, former editor of the *Chicago Tribune*, argues that the corporate takeover of the media has led to the "death of journalism."[29] And, aside from the pursuit of profit, even business commentators have been struck by how the media conglomerates are willing to censor and distort journalism to suit their corporate interests. Nowhere is this more evident than in the virtual blackout of critical coverage of the operations of the giant media and telecommunication firms, beyond what is produced in the business press and directed at investors. [30]

What is tragic—or absurd—is that the dominant perception of the "free press" still regards the government as the sole possible foe of freedom. That this notion of press freedom has been and is aggressively promoted by the giant media corporations should be no surprise, though that is rarely noted. Imagine if the federal government demanded that newspaper and broadcast journalism staffs be cut in half, that foreign bureaus be closed, and that news be tailored to suit the government's self-interests. There would be an outcry that would make the Alien & Sedition Acts, the Red Scares and Watergate seem like child's play. Yet when corporate America aggressively pursues the exact same policies, scarcely a murmur of dissent can be detected in the political culture.

With fewer journalists, limited budgets, low salaries and lower morale, the balance of power has shifted dramatically to the public relations industry, which seeks to fill the news media with coverage sympathetic to its clients. In the United States today, one expert estimates that there are 20,000 more PR agents than there are journalists.[31] Their job is to offer the news media sophisticated video press releases and press packets to fill the news hole, or contribute to the story that does fill the news hole.

The effects of this PR blitz on journalism can be seen on the two most important issues in U.S. politics in the 1990s: foreign trade and health care. These two issues are unusual because they provided clear public policy debates on the types of all important long-term issues (globalization of the economy and collapse of living standards and economic security) that professional journalism usually avoids. In the case of GATT and NAFTA, the large transnational corporations were almost unanimous and aggressive in their support of "free trade." While there was not the same unanimity in the business community regarding health care, the insurance industry had an enormous stake in maintaining control of the health sector. In both cases, these powerful interests were able to neutralize public opinion, even though, initially, based on personal experience, it was against GATT and NAFTA and for a single-payer health care system.

The demise of journalism was readily apparent in this process. In each of these issues, big business mounted sophisticated, multi-million-dollar PR campaigns to obfuscate the issues, confuse the public and, if not weaken the opposition to the business position, at least make it easier for powerful interests to ignore popular opinion. In effect, corporate America has been able to create its own "truth," and our news media seem unwilling or incapable of fulfilling the mission our society so desperately needs it to fill. And this is

ROBERT W. McCHESNEY

the likely pattern for the new global commercial journalism of the media giants.

Nor are newspaper and broadcast journalism the only casualties of a corporate-dominated, profit-motivated media system. The corporate takeover of much of U.S. magazine publishing has resulted in increased pressure upon editors to highlight editorial fare that pleases advertisers or that serves the political agenda of the corporate owners. By 1996 magazine editors were calling for a minimal standard to be voluntarily accepted by their corporate overlords that would respect some rudimentary notion of editorial integrity. A similar process is taking place with book publishing. After a wave of mergers and acquisitions, three of the world's four largest media giants now own the three largest global book publishers. At the retail end, U.S. bookselling is becoming highly concentrated into the hands of a few massive chains; nearly one-half of U.S. retail bookselling is accounted for by Barnes & Noble and Borders.[32] This corporatization of publishing has led to a marked shift to the political right in what types of books clear the corporate hurdles, as well as a trend to make books look "like everything else the mass media turn out." Book publishing, which not too long ago played an important role in stimulating public culture and debate, has largely abandoned that function, except to push the ideas of the corporate owners' favored interests. "The drive for profit," writes former Random House book editor Andre Schiffrin, "fits like an iron mask on our cultural output." He concludes that we may well have corporate "purveyors of culture who feel that one idea can fit all."[33]

Corporate concentration and profit-maximization have similarly disastrous effects upon music, radio, television and film. The stakes have been raised for commercial success. *Variety* concluded after a 1996 study of 164 films that "Films with budgets greater than $60 million are more likely to generate profit than cheaper pics."[34] One Hollywood movie producer notes that media mergers accelerate the existing trend toward "greater emphasis on the bottom line, more homogenization of content and less risk taking."[35] The one film genre that has proven least risky and has the greatest upside has been "action" fare. This is encouraged by the rapid rise in non-U.S. sales for Hollywood, such that they are now greater than domestic revenues. Violent fare, requiring less nuance than comedy or drama, is especially popular across markets. As one media executive said, "Kicking butt plays everywhere."[36] The other route for the corporate media giants to lessen risk is to specifically produce films that lend themselves to complementary merchandising of products: The revenues and profits generated here can often be equal or superior to those generated by traditional box-office sales or video rentals.[37] The ultimate result of this marriage of Hollywood and Madison Avenue came with the 1996 release of Time Warner's film *Space Jam*, based upon Nike shoe commercials, starring Bugs Bunny and Michael Jordan and directed by "the country's hottest director of commercials." As *Forbes* magazine puts it, "the real point of the movie is to sell, sell, sell." Time Warner "is looking to hawk up to $1 billion in toys, clothing, books, and sports gear based on the movie characters."[38] The implications for the "art" of filmmaking are evident.

Indeed, the commercialism of the media system

permeates every aspect of its being. The volume of advertising has increased rapidly in the United States over the past decade; U.S. television networks now broadcast 6,000 commercials per week, up 50 percent since 1983. As *Business Week* observes, "the buying public has been virtually buried alive in ads." Desperate to be seen and heard, advertisers are turning to new approaches, including "stamping their messages on everything that stands still."[39] To circumvent this commercial blizzard, and the consumer skepticism to traditional advertising, marketers are working to infiltrate entertainment. There are over two dozen consultancies in Los Angeles, for example, just to help link marketers with film and television producers, usually to get the marketer's product "placed" and promoted surreptitiously inside the programming.[40] "The connections between Madison Avenue and Hollywood have grown so elaborate," *Business Week* concludes, "that nothing is off-limits when studios and advertisers sit down to hammer out the marketing campaign."[41] Traditional notions of separation of editorial and commercial interests are weakening. Advertisers play a large and increasing role in determining media content. Media firms solicit the capital and input of advertising firms as they prepare programming. "Networks are happy to cater to advertisers who want a bigger role," one report stated.[42] A U.S. advertising executive expects advertisers everywhere to demand similar arrangements. "This is just a forerunner of what we are going to see as we get to 500 [television] channels. Every client will have their own programming tailored to their own needs, based on their ad campaign."[43]

THE INTERNET AND THE DIGITAL REVOLUTION

The rise of a global commercial media system is only one striking trend of the 1990s. The other is the rise of digital computer networks in general, and the Internet in particular. The logic of digital communication is that the traditional distinctions between telephony and all types of media are disappearing. Eventually, these industries will "converge," meaning firms active in one of them will by definition be capable of competing in the others. The present example of convergence is how cable and telephone companies can now offer each other's services. The Internet has opened up very important space for progressive and democratic communication, especially for activists hamstrung by traditional commercial media. This alone has made the Internet an extremely positive development. Yet whether one can extrapolate from this fact to see the Internet becoming the democratic medium for society writ large is another matter. The notion that the Internet will permit humanity to leapfrog over capitalism and corporate communication is in sharp contrast to the present rapid commercialization of the Internet.

Moreover, it will be many years before the Internet can possibly stake a claim to replace television as the dominant medium in the United States, and much longer elsewhere. This is due to bandwidth limitations, the cost of computers and access, and numerous, often complex, technical problems, all of which will keep Internet usage restricted. Rupert Murdoch, whose News Corporation has been perhaps the most aggressive of the media giants to explore the possibilities of cyberspace, states that establishing an information highway "is going to take longer than people think." He projects that

ROBERT W. McCHESNEY

it will take until at least 2010 or 2015 for a broadband network to reach fruition in the United States and western Europe, and until the middle of the 21st century for it to begin to dominate elsewhere.[44] Even Bill Gates, whose Microsoft is spending $400 million annually to become an Internet content provider, acknowledges that the Internet as mass medium "is going to come very slowly."[45] This is the clear consensus across the media and communications industries, and it explains the enormous investments in terrestrial broadcasting and digital satellite broadcasting that would be highly dubious if the broadband information highway was imminent. As MCA president Frank Biondi put it in 1996, media firms "don't even think of the Internet as competition."[46]

It is also unclear how firms will be able to make money by providing Internet content—and in a market-driven system this is the all-important question. Even the rosiest forecasts only see Internet advertising spending at $5 billion by 2000, representing only 2 or 3 percent of projected U.S. advertising spending that year. The media giants have all established websites and have the product and deep pockets to wait it out and establish themselves as the dominant players in cyberspace. They can also use their existing media to constantly promote their online ventures, and their relationships with major advertisers to bring them aboard their Internet ventures. In short, if the Internet becomes a viable commercial medium, there is a good chance that many of the media giants will be among the firms capable of capitalizing upon it. The other "winners" will probably be firms like Microsoft that have the resources to seize a portion of the market.

While the media firms do not face an immediate or direct threat from the Internet, such is not the case for computer software makers and telecommunication firms. The Internet is changing the basic nature of both their businesses, and both industries are turning their attention to incorporating the Internet into the heart of their activities. The eventual mergers and alliances that emerge will have tremendous impact upon global media as media firms are brought into the digital communication empires. This is speculative; it is also possible that the Internet itself will eventually be supplanted by a more commercially oriented digital communication network.

Due to the privatization and commercialization that is the cornerstone of the global market economy, we are in the midst of a sweeping reconstruction of global telecommunication from the system of non-profit national monopolies that dominated only 15 years ago. In the late 1990s the world's largest telecommunication firms have raced to put together global alliances.[47] When British Telecom purchased MCI for some $20 billion in November 1996 to form Concert, it signaled that alliances may turn into formal mergers. AT&T has allied with Singapore Telecom and four major European national firms to form World Partners; Sprint, Deutsche Telekom, and France Telecom have formed Global One.[48] *The Financial Times* predicts the endpoint may be "a handful of giants, straddling the world market."[49] MCI president Gerald H. Taylor concluded in 1996 that "There's probably going to be only four to six global gangs emerge over the next five years as all this sorts out."[50] Each of these global alliances strives to offer "one-stop shopping" of telephone, cellular, paging and Internet access services to the lucrative global business market.

By the logic of the market and convergence, we should expect that the global media oligopoly will gradually evolve into a far broader global communication oligopoly over the next one or two decades. BT-MCI already owns 13.5 percent of News Corporation and U.S. West has a large stake in Time Warner. The media giants will link with the handful of telecommunication "global gangs," and they all will strike deals with the leading computer firms. As one writer puts it, the goal of all the "info-communication" firms is "to ensure they are among what will end up being a handful of communication monoliths controlling both product and distribution networks in the future. . . . The basic aim of future M&A [mergers and acquisitions] is to control the transmission of three basic telecommunication products—voice, data and video."[51] In short, the Internet and digital communication networks will not undermine the development of a global communication oligopoly; rather, they will be an integral aspect of it. As a market-driven system, it will be built to satisfy the needs of businesses and affluent consumers. This is where the easiest profits are to be found.

Long ago—back in the Internet's ancient history, like 1994 and 1995—some Internet enthusiasts were so captivated by the technology's powers they regarded "cyberspace" as the end of corporate for-profit communication, because there people would be able to bypass the corporate sector and communicate globally with each other directly. That was then. Perhaps the most striking change in the late 1990s is how quickly the euphoria of those who saw the Internet as providing a qualitatively different and egalitarian type of journalism, politics, media and culture has faded. The indications are that the substantive content of this commercial media in the Internet, or any subsequent digital communication system, will look much like what currently exists. Indeed, advertisers and commercialism arguably have more influence over Internet content than anywhere else. Advertisers and media firms both aspire to make the Internet look more and more like commercial television, as that is a proven winner commercially. In December 1996 Microsoft reconfigured its huge online Microsoft Network to resemble a television format.[52] AT&T's director of Internet services says the Internet may become the ultimate advertising-driven medium: "If it's done well, you won't feel there's any tension between the consumerism and the entertainment."[53] Frank Beacham, who in 1995 enthused about the Internet as a public sphere outside corporate or governmental control, lamented one year later that the Internet was shifting "from being a participatory medium that serves the interests of the public to being a broadcast medium where corporations deliver consumer-oriented information. Interactivity would be reduced to little more than sales transactions and email."[54]

U.S. DEBATE ON COMMUNICATION POLICY

The analysis of the commercialization of the Internet is predicated upon the thorough absence of any political debate concerning how best to employ cyberspace. Were communication issues to become political issues, there is no reason why the Internet could not be redirected from its current main emphasis of serving business. Indeed, given the magnitude of the communication revolution and all the hype about its importance as the marker of our new age, it is remarkable how little communication and media policies figure in public debate. Fundamental decisions are being made, but even when they involve governments they tend to be made in semi-secrecy by private interests.

Historically the rise of crucial new communication technologies like broadcasting has generated national public debates over how best to deploy these resources. It was as a result of such debates, for example, that public systems of broadcasting were established to serve publicly determined goals, not to generate profit. These debates often took place among society's elites, but there has been periodic popular intervention. The extent to which there is non-elite participation into communication policymaking may be a barometer for the level of democracy in a society. As a rule of thumb, if certain forces thoroughly dominate a society's political economy they will thoroughly dominate its communication system, and the fundamental questions of how the communication system should be organized and for what purposes are not even subject to debate. So it is and so it has been with the Communist Party in various "people's republics," and, for the most part, with big business interests in the United States.

It is in the United States that the decline of public debate over communication is the most developed. Yet it might surprise most people to know that this is not because a love for commercial media is genetically encoded in persons born in the United States. It is an acquired taste. When radio broadcasting emerged in the 1920s few thought it had any commercial potential.⁵⁵ Many of broadcasting's pioneers were non-profit organizations interested in public service. It was only in the late 1920s that capitalists began to sense that through network operation and commercial advertising, radio broadcasting could generate substantial profits. Through their immense power in Washington, these commercial broadcasters were able to dominate the Federal Radio Commission. As a result, the scarce number of air channels were effectively turned over to them with no public and little congressional deliberation on the matter.

It was in the aftermath of this commercialization of the airwaves that elements of U.S. society coalesced into a broadcast reform movement that attempted to establish a dominant role for the non-profit and noncommercial sector in U.S. broadcasting. These opponents of commercialism came from education, religion, labor, civic organizations, women's groups, journalism, farmer's groups, civil libertarians, and intellectuals. The reformers attempted to tap into the intense public dislike for radio commercialism in the years before 1934, when Congress annually considered legislation for the permanent regulation of radio broadcasting. These reformers were explicitly radical; they argued that if private interests controlled the medium and their goal was profit, no amount of regulation or self-regulation could overcome the bias built into the system. Commercial broadcasting, the reformers argued, would downplay controversial, pro-working class and provocative public affairs programming and emphasize whatever fare would sell the most products for advertisers.

ROBERT W. McCHESNEY

The reform movement disintegrated after the passage of the Communications Act of 1934, which established the FCC. The 1930s reformers did not lose to the commercial interests on a level playing field, however. The commercial radio lobby dominated because it was able to keep most Americans ignorant or confused about the communication policy matters then under discussion in Congress through their control of key elements of the news media and their sophisticated public relations aimed at the remainder of the press and the public. In addition, commercial broadcasters became a force that few politicians wished to antagonize; almost all of the congressional leaders of broadcast reform in 1931-1932 were defeated in their re-election attempts, a fate not lost on those who entered the next Congress. With the defeat of the reformers, the industry's claim that commercial broadcasting was inherently democratic and American went unchallenged and became internalized in the political culture.

Thereafter the only legitimate manner to criticize U.S. broadcasting was to assert that it was uncompetitive or "excessively" commercial, and therefore needed moderate regulation to protect the public interest while not damaging the commercial viability of the industry. The basis for this "liberal" claim for regulation was that the scarce number of channels necessitated regulation, *not* that the capitalist basis of the industry was fundamentally flawed. This was a far cry from the criticism of the broadcast reformers in the 1930s, who argued that the problem was not simply one of lack of competition in the marketplace, as much as it was the rule of the marketplace per se. It also means that with the vast expansion in the number of channels in the current communication revolution, the scarcity argument has lost its power and liberals are at a loss to withstand the deregulatory juggernaut.

This constricted range of policy debate was the context for the development of subsequent communication technologies including facsimile, FM radio, and television in the 1940s. That the communication corporations had first claim to these technologies was not disputed, even by public-service-minded New Dealers. In comparison to the public debate over radio in the 1930s, there was almost no public debate concerning alternative ways to develop these technologies. By the 1940s and thereafter, liberals knew the commercial basis of the system was inviolate, and they merely tried to carve out a nonprofit sector on the margins. (This was problematical, since whenever these nonprofit niches were seen as blocking profitable expansion, their future was on thin ice.)

The marginalization of public service values in U.S. communication debates—indeed the elimination of political debates over communication—explains the woeful history of U.S. public radio and television. The defeat of the broadcast reform movement in 1934 led to what might be called the Dark Ages of U.S. public broadcasting. If the 1930s reformers sought a system where the dominant sector was nonprofit and noncommercial, all future advocates of public broadcasting had to accept that the system was established primarily to benefit the commercial broadcasters, and any public stations would have to find a niche on the margins, where they would not threaten the existing or potential profitability of the commercial interests.

This made public broadcasting in the U.S. fundamentally different from Britain or Canada, or nearly any other nation with a comparable political economy. Whereas the BBC and the CBC regarded their mandate as providing a service to the entire nation, the U.S. public broadcasters realized that they could only survive politically by not taking listeners or viewers away from the commercial broadcasters. The function of the public or educational broadcasters, then, was to provide such programming as was unprofitable for the commercial broadcasters to produce. At the same time, however, politicians and government officials hostile to public broadcasting also insisted that public broadcasting remain within the same ideological confines as the commercial system. This encouraged U.S. public broadcasting after 1935 to emphasize elite cultural programming at the expense of generating a large following. In short, since 1935 public broadcasting in the United States has been in a no-win situation.

The major function of nonprofit broadcasting in the United States from 1920 to 1960 was, in fact, to pioneer new sections of the electromagnetic spectrum when the commercial interests did not yet view them as profitable. Thus it was educational broadcasters who played an enormous role in developing AM broadcasting in the 1920s, and then FM radio and even UHF television in the 1940s and 1950s. In each case, once it became clear that money could be made, the educators were displaced and capitalists seized the reins. Arguably, too, this looks like the fate of the Internet, which had been pioneered as a public service by the nonprofit sector with government subsidies until capital decided to take over and relegate the pioneers to the margins. The 1930s broadcast reformers were well aware of this tendency and refused to let the FCC push them into new technologies where there would be no access to the general public. After 1935, the proponents of public broadcasting had no choice in the matter. (In many cases, such as the Internet, satellites and digital communication, these technologies were developed through research funds provided by the federal government. Once the technologies proved profitable, however, they were turned over to private interests with negligible compensation.)

Even with these limitations, the commercial broadcasters were wary of public broadcasting and fought it tooth and nail well into the 1960s. After many halting starts, Congress passed the Public Broadcasting Act of 1967, which led to the creation of the Corporation for Public Broadcasting, and soon thereafter of PBS and NPR. The commercial broadcasters finally agreed not to oppose public broadcasting, primarily because they believed the new public system could be responsible for doing the unprofitable cultural and public affairs programming that critics were constantly lambasting them for neglecting. There was a catch, however. The initial plan to have the CPB funded by a sales tax on the purchase of new radio sets and television sets, somewhat akin to the BBC method, was dropped, thus denying public broadcasting a stable source of income necessary for planning as well as editorial autonomy. At the outset it was determined that Americans would have a public system, but it would be severely handicapped. We would have only a system the commercial broadcasters would permit.

Although U.S. public broadcasting has produced

some good fare, the system has been supremely compromised by its structural basis, and it is farcical in comparison to the powerful public service systems of Europe. Indeed, in international discussions of public broadcasting, the term "PBS-style system" is invoked to refer to a public system that is marginal and ineffective. It is the fate that the BBC, CBC and others wish to avoid.

The funding system is the primary culprit. The U.S. government only provides around 15 percent of the revenues; public stations depend on corporate donations, foundation grants, and listener/viewer contributions for the balance. In effect, this has made PBS and NPR stations commercial enterprises, and it has given the large corporations that dominate its subsidy tremendous influence over public broadcasting content, in a manner that violates the fundamental principles of public broadcasting. It has also encouraged the tendency to appeal to an affluent audience, rather than a working-class audience, because upscale viewers/listeners have far more disposable income. Ironically, it is this well-heeled base of support that gives public broadcasting the leverage it has in negotiations for federal monies, as much as any argument for "public" media. If the federal subsidy were fully eliminated, the bias toward corporate interests and an upper-income target audience would be magnified.

THE U.S. TELECOMMUNICATIONS ACT OF 1996

With the digital revolution, the technical and legal boundaries between broadcasting and telephony in the 1934 Communications Act have broken down. Indeed, the barriers between all forms of communication are breaking down, and communication laws everywhere are becoming outdated. Congress passed, and President Clinton signed into law, the Telecommunications Act of 1996 to replace the 1934 law. The overarching purpose of the 1996 Telecommunications Act is to deregulate all communication industries and to permit the market, not public policy, to determine the course of the information highway and the communications system. It is widely considered to be one of the three or four most important federal laws of this generation.

Even by the minimal standards of the 1934 Act, the debate surrounding the 1996 Telecommunications Act was a farce. Some of the law was actually written by the lobbyists for the communication firms it affects. The only "debate" was whether broadcasters, long-distance companies, local telephone providers, or cable companies would get the inside track in the deregulatory race. Consistent with the pattern set in the middle 1930s, the primacy of corporate control and the profit motive was a given. The range of legitimate debate extended from that of Newt Gingrich, who argued profits are synonymous with public service, to that of Vice-President Al Gore, who argued that there are public interest concerns the marketplace cannot resolve, but that can only be addressed once the profitability of the dominant corporate sector has been assured. The historical record with communication regulation indicates that although the Gore position can be gussied up, once the needs of corporations are given primacy, the public interest will invariably be pushed to the margins.

This situation exists for many of the same reasons that the broadcast reformers were demolished in the 1930s. Politicians may favor one sector over another in the battle to cash in on the highway, but they cannot oppose the cashing-in process without risking their political careers. Both the Democratic and Republican parties have strong ties to the large communication firms and industries, and the communication lobbies are among the most feared, respected and well endowed of all that seek favors on Capitol Hill. The only grounds for political independence in this case would be if there were an informed and mobilized citizenry ready to do battle for alternative policies. But where would citizens get informed? Only through the news media, where news coverage is minimal and restricted to the range of legitimate debate, which, in this case, means almost no debate at all. That is why the Telecommunications Act was covered (rather extensively) as a *business* story, not a *public policy* story. "I have never seen anything like the Telecommunications Bill," one career lobbyist observed. "The silence of public debate is deafening. A bill with such astonishing impact on all of us is not even being discussed."[56]

In sum, the debate over communications policy is restricted to elites and those with serious financial stakes in the outcome. It does not reflect well on the caliber of U.S. participatory democracy, but it is capitalist democracy at its best. The politicians of both parties promised the public that the Telecommunications Act would provide a spurt in high-paying jobs and intense market competition in communications, a "digital free-for-all," as one liberal Democrat put it. Even a cursory reading of the business press at the same time would reveal that those who benefited from the law knew these claims to be half-truths or outright lies. These are oligopolistic industries that strongly discourage all but the most judiciously planned competition. It is more likely that deregulation will lead to merger activity, increased concentration, and continued "downsizing." And, as the U.S. 1996 Telecommunications Act "unleashes" the U.S.-based transnational media and communication firms to grow through mergers and acquisitions with minimal fear of regulatory intervention, this effectively gives the green light to further consolidation of the global market these firms dominate. As such, the U.S. Telecommunications Act is to some extent a global law.

THE MARKET AS CIVIC RELIGION

In the end, the case for commercialized communication relies upon the ideology of the infallible marketplace, a virtual civic religion in the United States and in the world in the 1990s. The argument goes that the self-regulating market is the most perfect, rational and equitable mechanism for regulating social affairs known to humankind; efforts to interfere with it by governments or outside agencies will only reduce its sublime powers. (ABC correspondent John Stossel captures this vision perfectly: "I have come to believe that markets are magical and the best protectors of the consumer. It is my job to explain the beauties of the free market."[57]) Unless media activists—and anti-corporate activists in general—deal with this notion of the market directly and debunk it, they have little chance of success. This pro-market argument remains infallible only to the extent that it is a religion based on faith, not a political theory subject to inquiry and examination.

The case for the market often rests upon a mythological presentation of pure competition, where there are an infinite number of small entrepreneurs battling to serve the public by lowering prices and improving quality in constant ferocious competition. This vision of capitalism, so prevalent in the rhetoric of the Thatchers, Kemps, Pinochets and Friedmans of the world, bears little resemblance to the genuine article. This vision of capitalism is any corporation's worst nightmare, and successful capitalists invariably and quickly move to reduce their risk by increasing their size and reducing the threat of direct competition. Accordingly, most major markets tend to become oligopolies, in which a relative handful of firms dominate activity and create severe "barriers-to-entry" to prevent new competitors. In terms of pricing, output, and profits, oligopolistic industries resemble pure monopolies far more closely than they do the mythical competitive market. Capitalists revel in the rhetoric of the free market, but the reality is one of highly concentrated, unaccountable economic power. And in few areas is this more true than in the advertising, media and telecommunication industries.

Beyond the mythology, the market is in fact a highly flawed regulatory mechanism for a democracy. In markets, one's income and wealth determine one's power. It is a system of "one dollar, one vote," rather than "one person, one vote." Viewed in this manner, the market is more a plutocratic mechanism than a democratic one. In communication this means that the emerging system is tailored to the needs of business and the affluent. Nor do markets "give the people what they want" as much as they "give the people what they want within the range of what is most profitable to produce and/or in the political interests of the producers." This is a far narrower range than what people might enjoy choosing from, or should be able to choose from if a democracy culture is to be nurtured. Thus, in the case of 1930s broadcasting, many Americans may well have been willing to pay for an advertising-free system, but this was a choice that was unprofitable for the dominant commercial interests, so it was not offered in the marketplace. More recently, a 1995 advertising industry survey showed that 2/3 of U.S. adults preferred that there be *no* advertising on the Internet. This, too, was a choice the market dismissed as irrelevant.[58] Beyond communication, issues of clear importance to the bulk of the population such as the need for universal education, health care, employment, and environmental quality cannot be addressed adequately by the market. In fact, these public goods must be provided by the state, and they are often opposed by business interests as unwarranted intrusions into their control over the political economy.

In addition, markets, driven as they are by the need to generate profit, cannot address their unintended consequences that do not affect the bottom line, or what economists term externalities. Some externalities, like the public satisfaction at seeing an attractive garden outside a private factory or office building, are positive, but many, like pollution, are negative. It is worth noting that media have externalities too. Positive ones include the increasing political interest and knowledge that results from public affairs programming. Negative externalities include the adverse social effects of programming trivia and mindless violence. In a democratic society, these externalities cannot be ignored.

They must be discussed and debated in the political sphere, with efforts made to emphasize the positive ones and discourage the negative ones.

At the individual level, too, the market is a superficial indicator of human wants and needs. Considerable research points to the fact that the "social values" of love, family and friendships outrank "material values" of economic security and success in providing the basis for a happy life and self-esteem. Yet markets are ill-equipped to address social values except to exploit them, often perversely, in advertising messages to sell commodities. To the extent that markets encourage some of our worst traits (selfishness and greed) and discourage some of our best traits (generosity and compassion), they arguably increase human unhappiness.[59] "What we crave most of all," Norman Solomon observes, "genuine love, joy, community, peace of mind—can't be bought at any price."[60]

Much of the ideological strength of markets as a regulatory mechanism for the media comes from the metaphor of the "marketplace of ideas." The image conjured by this term is one where as long as there is no government interference, all varieties of ideas will blossom under democracy's sun, with the truest ideas growing tallest. The market is assumed to be a neutral and value-free regulatory mechanism. In fact, for the reasons mentioned above, a commercial "marketplace" of ideas has a strong bias toward rewarding ideas supportive of the status quo and marginalizing socially dissident views. Markets tend to reproduce social inequality economically, politically *and* ideologically. The metaphor serves to mystify the actual corporate domination of our communication system and therefore provides the commercial interests with a valuable shield from rightful public criticism and participation in the policymaking process. As David Kairys has noted, in the 19th century the image of the market was used to expand the range of freedom of speech. In the late 20th century, the image of free speech has been used to expand the range and power of the market. So it has been that much of the "expansion" of the U.S. First Amendment in the past generation has been to protect commercial speech (e.g. advertising) and profit-making activities from government regulation, effectively making such "speech" part of the constitution and therefore off-limits to political consideration.[61] (In 1996, for an example of what we can expect from corporate "free speech," food-processing companies filed suits claiming they could not be required to reveal the contents of their foods on their labels because that violated their First Amendment rights. Their cases are still pending.[62]) This myopic interpretation of the First Amendment, where markets can do no wrong, has had the ironic effect of expanding formal free speech while helping to shrink the effective range and quality of political debate.[63]

At its worst, the commercial marketplace of ideas puts an Orwellian spin on the notions of the free marketplace of ideas inspired by John Milton and John Stuart Mill. Truth, as such, loses its intrinsic meaning. It is less something to be respected and argued over than it is something to be auctioned off to the highest bidder; it is bought and sold. In the commercial marketplace of ideas, something becomes "true" if you can get people to believe it. And one attempts to get people to believe something to profit off them. For example, the notion that drinking a particular beer will make one more ath-

ROBERT W. McCHESNEY

letic, sexually attractive and have more friends is patently false. But if one "convinces" people of it and they purchase the beer, it becomes true and the creator of the message is duly rewarded. (Someone who actually told the truth would be fired.) This spirit permeates conventional political discourse as well, as much of campaign research is predicated upon finding which decontextualized facts, half-truths, and outright lies can be successfully deployed against an opponent. As this notion of "truth" is generalized, the sense of a moral common ground declines, and the function of communication becomes to advance narrowly defined self-interest. The implications for democracy are disastrous.

In communication, as noted before, the profession of journalism is predicated upon the dictum that news is not something that should be influenced by market factors. News should not be bought and sold. The moment journalism acknowledges that it is predominantly influenced by the needs of advertisers or owners rather than the public, it instantly loses its legitimacy. The canons of professional journalism are fairly flexible, however, and commercial values have always been incorporated into them, albeit discreetly. This is in the process of unraveling. The commercial blitzkrieg into every nook and cranny of U.S. culture, from schools to sport to museums to movie theaters to the Internet, has lessened traditional distinctions of public service from commercialism. This has combined with the bottom-line desires of the media firms to produce the "tabloidization" of mainstream journalism over the past decade. Although this commercialization of news has received superficial comment and criticism, there are almost no sustained efforts by journalists or mainstream critics to explain why the phenomenon exists in the first place and what could be done to address the problem structurally. It is, in fact, the organic response of corporate media to the organizing logic of the commercial marketplace of ideas: if the desired target audience consumes it, if it is relatively inexpensive to produce, if powerful interests are not affected negatively, and if advertisers and owners approve of it—i.e. if it is profitable—it is news. Hence we see massive quantities of O.J. Simpson, celebrity lifestyles, incidents of bizarre personal behavior and plane crashes, but minuscule coverage of public affairs outside of narrow elite opinion and little scrutiny of secret (and secretive) government agencies or powerful economic institutions.

But what about the notion that the entertainment media—which have no public service mandate outside of the market—"give the people what they want," due to their desire to maximize profits? This, too, is flawed. If there is anything people do not want, it is commercial messages permeating films, television programs, sports and every other conceivable venue. Indeed, for much of the entertainment media, the primary goal is to "give the advertisers what they want," not the people. And the needs of advertisers and audiences are by no means synonymous.

Moreover, this notion that the commercial entertainment media "give the people what they want" reduces a complex process of commercial cultural production to a simplistic one of all-powerful audiences barking out orders to obedient media giants. The commercial media certainly consider some aspects of audience demand, but that is only one of many factors

ROBERT W. McCHESNEY

involved in production. In the final analysis, commercial media firms produce that which is most profitable and in their interests. When people consume from the options provided, the media giants then state that they are satisfying audience demand. If some find the offerings imbecilic, the argument goes, that is because the people are morons who demand such tripe. But this is a circular argument, since there is no proof that this range of choices conforms to something innate to the audience. "We are told that this is what the public wants," Albert Camus observed in a 1944 newspaper article on media ethics. "No. This is not what the public wants. This is what the public has been taught to want . . . which isn't the same thing."[64] For example, were people not exposed to an incessant diet of violent fare, is it possible that there would be a smaller market for it? And, to the extent that this is the case, is it wise social policy to permit media giants and exclusively commercial values to dictate the media curriculum?

A major reason for the success of the market ideologically—in communication and in society writ large—is the notion that, no matter how weak the market may be, there is no superior alternative. The collapse of the various alternatives to capitalism, it is said—meaning not only authoritarian Soviet style communist regimes but also social democratic regimes as in Sweden—all point to the fact that there is no other route than the market. We are at the "end of history." Yet this seems more apologia than explanation. In the media, for example, there are impressive examples of public service communication. More broadly, the collapse of social democracy had less to do with the weaknesses of socialism, per se, as much as the inability of capitalism to accommodate a powerful, democratic public sector concerned as much with common people as with business. This, apparently, is a prospect that at a certain point a market-driven political economy cannot countenance. And, for that reason, those committed to democracy must push to establish a political economy that is compatible with democracy. If the market cannot deliver, it must be replaced or its powers curtailed.

Nor should the market's power be exaggerated. The market may well be a "civic religion," but faith in the market decreases the further one looks down the social pecking order. For much of the U.S. population the turn to the unbridled "free market" in the 1980s and 1990s has been a largely negative experience, and for a significant minority the turn has been disastrous. It is the "talking classes," the upper class, the upper middle class, and the intellectuals who have become the most enthralled with the market's genius, and the most willing to throw social welfare programs overboard. In their conceit they assume to speak for all. Even the self-proclaimed Christian right has found it difficult to sell free market ideology to its lower-middle-class and working-class adherents; these folks may be "conservative" on some issues, but they know firsthand the importance of unemployment insurance, social security, Medicare and welfare. Moreover, many so-called conservatives, Christian and otherwise, may well be open to arguments that it is the market, commercialism and advertising, as much as any liberal tomfoolery, that are laying waste to families, communities, and traditional values. Therefore, to accept the market as off-limits to political debate, is to agree to eliminate political debate in any meaningful sense. This plays directly into the hands of the

ROBERT W. McCHESNEY

powers that be. And as the social order is in various degrees of crisis nationally and globally, that would leave the domain of providing criticism of the status quo to various fundamentalists and ultra-nationalists, who blame democracy for the market's flaws and threaten to reduce humanity to untold barbarism.

If not the market, what then would be a truly democratic manner to generate communication policymaking, especially in an era of technological upheaval like ours? The historical record points to one basic principle: citizens must determine the nature of their communication system through full and open political debate—precisely the opposite of what led up to the passage of the U.S. Telecommunications Act. Is such public participation an absurd idea? Hardly. In the late 1920s, Canada, noting the rapid commercialization of the U.S. and Canadian airwaves, convened precisely such a public debate over broadcasting that included public hearings in 25 cities in all nine provinces. The final decision to develop a nonprofit system was adopted three years later after a further period of active debate.[65]

Putting democracy before profits in communication policymaking also means that the pace of technological innovation can be brought under rational control, with long-term social, cultural and political consequences taken into consideration. In a manner similar to market externalities, every major communication technology has significant unintended and unanticipated social consequences—consider television for example—and democratic policymaking should aspire to account for them to the best of our abilities. Even those who study communication or who work in the field do not really have any idea what our society will be like when everything is digitized and computerized. "Everything will be different," FCC chairman Reed Hundt admits. "The change is so extreme that many people have not grasped it."[66] For every utopian celebration of computer technology there are numerous dystopian visions of an atomized, inhumane and anti-social future, which, given the more realistic social premises upon which these dystopias are based, may be more plausible in their projections. These are the types of complex issues that need to be publicly addressed and resolved, and soon: we need to look before we leap. Yet these are precisely the types of issues in which the market—blinded by the pursuit of profit—has no interest.

THE RIGHT WING ATTACK ON THE "LIBERAL" MEDIA

Although the effects of corporate ownership, the pursuit of profit, or the impact of advertising on the media rarely emerge as an issue in mainstream U.S. political discourse, this does not mean that the political culture lacks any debate over the merits of the existing media. There is a widely publicized discussion over whether the media have a "liberal" or even left-wing, anti-business bias. This has been a common theme among U.S. conservatives since at least the 1960s. It was made most recently by Republican presidential candidate Bob Dole to explain why voters were not flocking to his cause. Apparently voters were now believing the same "liberal" media in 1996 that they dismissed categorically in the 1994 Republican landslide.

What is the basis of this argument? In conservative analysis, the only independent variable that affects

ROBERT W. McCHESNEY

news content is the political bias of reporters and editors, which conservatives regard as decidedly liberal.[67] Conservatives point to surveys indicating that working journalists tend to vote Democratic far more frequently than they vote Republican. A Freedom Forum survey of 139 members of the Washington press corps, for example, showed that over 80 percent of them voted for Bill Clinton in 1992. Nor is the notion of journalists as liberals historically farfetched. As Herbert Gans has observed, the ideology of professional journalism encompasses the political values of the Progressive era, with its sympathy for competitive capitalism and its distrust of plutocracy. As such, journalism has tended to lean toward the liberal wing of legitimate public opinion in the United States, and has attracted to journalism those who shared this perspective.

But does this mean, therefore, that the U.S. media have a liberal or even left-wing bias and are hostile to the interests of business? Not really. The conservative argument is problematic on several counts and fatally flawed by one basic error. It is problematic because it tends to have a shifting and elusive definition of liberalism. In most examples, conservatives point to liberals' positions on "social issues" such as women's rights, gay rights, and civil liberties as the litmus test for whether one is liberal or conservative. Often journalists have fairly conservative positions on class issues of trade, taxation and government social spending, especially as one climbs to the high-paying ranks of the elite journalists. Moreover, it is unclear exactly why opposing mandatory drug-testing or the outlaw of abortion or mandatory pledges of allegiance to the flag are necessarily "liberal" positions. Conservatism, at its best, has traditionally been opposed to state intervention into the private affairs of individuals. But contemporary U.S. conservatives are a different breed. The state can have carte blanche in regulating some behavior, monitoring some people's activities, and having an enormous penal system. It can also provide ample corporate subsidies through military spending, taxation and numerous other mechanisms. Indeed, contemporary U.S. conservatives do not show the slightest concern about the enormous and unaccountable power held by large corporations, although their frequently invoked heroes like Adam Smith were well aware of the problems of concentrated wealth and corporate ownership. For the new breed of "conservatives," the only apparent hard-and-fast principle is that the state cannot interfere with the prerogatives of business and the wealthy, nor use monies in ways that benefit primarily the poor and the working class.

Moreover, to the extent that journalists are liberal, it is a liberalism that is rigidly defined by being on the "left" side of the spectrum of elite opinion. It is a liberalism thoroughly committed to capitalism and existing social relations. The conservatives err in collapsing liberals and radicals into a single montage of leftishness that ranges unambiguously from Bill Clinton to Subcomandante Marcos of the Zapatistas. There is no place for a genuine class-based principled left position except as caricature. In truth, the real chasm in U.S. politics and media culture is between those within the range of elite opinion—the conservatives and the liberals—and those outside it, who tend to regard the world in terms of class power and are, by definition, radicals. In addition to col-

ROBERT W. McCHESNEY

lapsing radicals into the liberal branch of elite opinion, conservative media critics argue that these liberals/radicals are actually society's ruling class, and that they—the conservatives bankrolled by great wealth and business interests—are the oppressed "populist" sector of society. For conservative "populists" to succeed, it is mandatory that the "alternative" to their position not be socialism or labor, but, rather, the elitist corporate liberalism of the U.S. Democratic Party and *The New York Times.*

This is where conservative criticism of the "liberal" media strikes close to home, and where it can generate sympathy. Conservatives are able to tap into genuine resentment against a corporate media system whose public face is that of arrogant millionaire celebrity journalists who presume to speak on behalf of the public. But conservative media criticism tends to degenerate into a "heads I win, tails you lose" mode, where anything in the news media critical of favored conservative politicians or anything insufficiently harsh toward the liberal enemy is ascribed to journalistic bias. There is never the slightest attempt to have a single standard based upon principle; it is all about jawboning better coverage of right-wing politics.

In fact, journalists are almost never radicals, but some genuine progressives have survived and done good work over the years by taking advantage of what journalistic autonomy has existed. This has proven ever more difficult in recent years, as elite opinion has moved rightward, bringing with it journalistic "liberalism." That Bill Clinton, whose administration has arguably been as pro-corporate as any in recent history, is now presented as the standard-bearer of "liberalism" is the clearest sign possible of how stunted the nature of U.S. political debate has become. (Indeed, for every dollar the "anti-business" Democratic Party received in campaign contributions from organized labor in 1996, it received nearly ten dollars from corporations.[68]) Under the commercial constraints and corporate cutbacks facing journalists, they are hard pressed to interject any politics that might antagonize their bosses. For the most part, to the extent that journalists do determine the news, they are fighting an uphill battle with their sources and the public relations industry for control of the news. In short, the autonomy of journalism has been undermined.

Another critical factor in moving journalism rightward has been the extremely well-financed right-wing media and ideological campaign of the past two decades. With lavish funding from a dozen major conservative foundations, including those of Bradley, Scaife, and Olin, conservative groups have developed a very sophisticated PR apparatus to funnel conservative positions and stories into the media.[69] To no small extent the cult of the market and the contempt for government as a progressive agency has been brewed in this kitchen. Nothing remotely close to this exists on the political left. Well-paid conservative "experts" voice opinions in the media on nearly any subject that arises. Conservative pundits dominate TV and radio discussion programs, paired with centrists who are quite comfortable in the corridors of corporate power. It is ironic that the numerous and vocal TV and radio conservatives simultaneously inundate the public with stories of how "liberal" and "biased" the media are. By contrast, it is nearly impossible to find even token left criticism of the press in the mainstream media.

To some extent, the ample publicity the mainstream media give to the criticism that journalists are liberals is necessary for the system; it provides the "loyal opposition" to show that the journalism is feisty and democratic. It flatters journalists by saying that journalists are *the* important figures in determining the news, and their problem is that they are too hard on corporations and the military—the powerful—and too sympathetic to the poor, minorities, women and the environment. That is hardly the worst thing a journalist could be told, whereas the converse would be completely unacceptable. As Noam Chomsky has stated, journalists almost *have* to be the "liberals" in a media system for it be credible. In this sense, if conservative media criticism did not exist it would have to be invented.

Left-wing media criticism is very different. By suggesting that journalists are relatively powerless before the institutional factors that create a tepid, ineffectual journalism that promotes elite interests, it raises doubt about the legitimacy of the entire corporate media enterprise. So it is almost nowhere to be found. When left criticism is mentioned in the mainstream media, it is usually in conjunction with conservative criticism. At that point, mainstream journalists usually proclaim, "See, we're being shot at from both sides, so we must be doing it right." The "shot at from both sides" thesis is absurd. All media systems generate criticism from different parts of the political spectrum. Even the Nazi media probably had critics who thought it was insufficiently nationalistic or too soft on Jews and communists. Does this mean the Nazis were "doing it right?" Of course not.

The way to analyze media accurately is through hard examination based on evidence.

This leads to the fundamental error in the conservative notion of the "liberal" media: it posits that editors and journalists have almost complete control over what goes into the news. Thus, because journalists tend to be liberal, the news is liberal. In conservative "analysis," the institutional factors of corporate ownership, profit-motivation, and advertising-support have no effect on media content. At its worst, this conservative criticism is a variant of traditional far right-wing social analysis that neglects the study of social institutions and attempts to identify scapegoats to explain unsatisfactory performance. (This approach is even more apparent—and implausible—in conservative critiques of the mindless materialistic values of entertainment fare. Even though there is no cast of professionals to protect the public interest from commercial values, the roles of profit motivation and advertising are conspicuously absent. In the place of liberal journalists, it is immoral counterculture types from the 1960s who have seized control of Hollywood, pushing unwholesome and often unprofitable fare upon the public, largely unbeknownst to owners and advertisers.[70]) But virtually no scholarship supports this contention, even by mainstream analysts unsympathetic to the left. The notion that journalism can regularly produce a product that violates the fundamental interests of media owners and advertisers and do so with impunity simply has no evidence behind it. It is absurd.

For an analogy, think of the press system in the old U.S.S.R. during the post-Stalinist years. The top Soviet journalists, working for *Pravda*, *Izvestia*, and Tass, were

ROBERT W. McCHESNEY

relatively free from direct harassment and censorship by the Communist Party and the state, their employers and subsidizers. The top Soviet journalists were also, in general, probably liberal on issues of civil liberties, at least by Soviet standards. They may well have represented the "liberal" wing of Communist Party opinion. Yet while there were debates in the Soviet press, the debates never countenanced positions outside of leading factions in the Communist Party, and while corrupt or incompetent commissars could receive a beating in the press, communism per se was exempt from criticism. In those rare instances when a Soviet journalist overstepped his or her bounds, that journalist would be demoted or punished in a more severe manner. A few incidents such as this sent a clear message to those who remained, and who wished to succeed. By the time journalists had reached the highest echelon of the Soviet media, they had generally internalized the necessary journalism values to succeed, either giving them no thought or regarding them as benevolent and proper. Although the United States is a vastly freer society than the old Soviet Union, in key respects this is the nature of a U.S. newsroom, journalists' relationship to owners' and advertisers' values, and journalism's relationship to capitalism and elite opinion.

The true nature of this relationship of U.S. news media to elite power was revealed in an unusually clear light when the *San Jose Mercury News* published a remarkable three-part series in 1996 suggesting that the CIA had worked with crack dealers in Los Angeles to help subsidize the CIA-backed and directed Contra war against the Nicaraguan government in the 1980s. If accurate, the piece called into question the continuance of the CIA and a media system that has failed to question it throughout its history. Although the *Mercury News* series may not have been perfect, other investigations, like the ones conducted by Britain's ITV and *The Independent*, suggest it may have understated the involvement of the CIA with the narcotics trade. Yet the elite news media—e.g. the "liberal" *New York Times*, *Washington Post* and *Los Angeles Times*, which generally serve as the gatekeepers for what news stories are "legitimate" for the balance of the media— ignored the story initially. Then, when that tack became impossible due to pressure mostly from the Congressional Black Caucus and the African-American community, they mounted a full scale assault to discredit the story. Indeed, with but a couple of noteworthy exceptions, the elite media have never investigated the CIA to any extent, despite the fact that, by the ostensible standards of journalism, this enormous top secret government agency is a natural target for inquiry by a free press. Moreover, there has been documented evidence of CIA involvement with drug dealing, political assassinations and dubious fascist and far right anti-democratic groups for decades.[71]

Why then is the CIA never covered in our news media? The CIA's primary function is to advance U.S. interests surreptitiously and illegally around the world. U.S. interests are defined by elites as being synonymous with corporate interests. The purpose therefore is to create a political environment conducive to profitable investment opportunities, regardless of the social cost. Although some in the political and economic elite may dispute CIA tactics, all agree it is a necessary agency. To elites, this is not a subject that

ROBERT W. McCHESNEY

is to be debated by the unwashed public that may not appreciate the need for such an agency. And since there is no reason for people to be informed and concerned about an issue best left to elites, this is not a subject to be examined by the press. Just as no explicit policing was necessary to keep the Soviet elite media from examining the KGB, no directive needs to be sent down from corporate owners and managers notifying editors and reporters to lay off the CIA; through a variety of organizational mechanisms it is merely internalized as "natural," "appropriate" and "responsible."

Hence, in attempting to discredit the *Mercury News* story, the elite news media effectively stated that they needed to be presented with virtually incontrovertible evidence of CIA guilt before they would even consider launching a serious investigation. Such an evidentiary standard is nonsensical; if applied across the board it would be nearly impossible to find any subject for journalistic examination. In reality, this is the abdication of journalism in service to elite interests. Those journalists who continue with the crazy idea that the CIA should be investigated are dismissed with ridicule as paranoids, and those who do so know full well that they are reducing, if not terminating, their chances at professional success. The most successful journalists internalize the notion that wanting to investigate the CIA is a kooky idea if they even consider the subject. Conservative media critics approve whole-heartedly of keeping the CIA out of the public eye, since their true concern is to protect corporate power, not to protect the public from "big government." When pieces such as the *San Jose Mercury News* series appear, their job is to howl about liberal bias to discredit the piece and demand that journalists back down. In cases like these, where the subject deals directly with the legitimacy of elite and corporate power—and where elite opinion is unified—the conservatives find themselves in bed with their "liberal" adversaries.

In fact, conservative media critics understand the crucial importance of media ownership and control for determining media content far better than they let on in their public pronouncements. They highlight editors and journalists as the decisive independent variable because they are the one factor that can take journalism away from serving explicitly corporate interests. One could argue that the entire conservative media project is predicated on smashing journalistic autonomy and having a feeble journalism that kowtows not only to the interests of media owners and advertisers, but the wealthy and powerful in general. Do you think this extreme? When Jesse Helms led an effort to purchase CBS in the 1980s, his rallying slogan was "We want to become Dan Rather's boss." And no less a conservative media critic than Newt Gingrich urged media owners and the largest advertisers in 1995 to crack the whip on the "socialists" in the newsroom, to see that the news conforms to the owners' and the advertisers' political agenda.[72]

This explains why conservatives are so obsessed with destroying, or at least intimidating, nonprofit and noncommercial broadcasting. They realize full well that the marketplace implicitly censors journalism to keep it within the ever-narrowing range they consider acceptable. Conservatives live in fear of a journalism not constrained by the profit imperative and commercial support. It is true that much of public broadcasting journalism and public affairs programming is indistinguishable from commercial journalism. Nonetheless, on occasion stories slip through and programs get produced that would never clear a commercial media hurdle. This is especially true on public radio and with some of the more progressive community stations that would suffer the most without any federal grant money.

The right-wing assault on journalism and public broadcasting is not an isolated or exceptional phenomenon. It is part and parcel of a wholesale attack on all those institutions that possess some autonomy from the market and the rule of capital. Thus public libraries and public education are being primed for privatization and an effective renunciation of the democratic principles upon which they were developed. Advertising-supported schools and schooling-for-profit—notions regarded as obscene only a decade ago—are moving to the center of education policy debates. The closest case to public broadcasting is that of higher education. Here, too, the right prattles on about leftist thought police and politically correct speech codes when, in fact, the dominant trend among U.S. universities is increasingly to turn to professional education and skew research toward the market. In short, the right wishes to eliminate the autonomy of the university and see it thoroughly integrated into the capitalist economy. To the extent that this is accomplished, as with public broadcasting or public education, our ability to generate a democratic and critical debate concerning our future is reduced. The reign of capital becomes more entrenched. Commercial values become ever more "natural."

By the logic of the public sphere, the crucial structural factor for democratic media is to have the dominant portion of the communication system removed from the control of business and the support of advertising. The government will have to subsidize some portion of the public sphere, and at the same time devise policies that encourage the growth of a nonprofit, noncommercial public sphere independent of state authority. There are justified reservations about government involvement with communication. The purpose of policymaking, then, should be to determine how to deploy these technologies to create a decentralized, accountable, nonprofit and noncommercial sector, which could provide a viable service to the entire population. And in times like these, when revolutionary technologies like the Internet hold extraordinary potential for democratic communication, it is imperative that we prevent the present appropriation of digital communication to suit the needs of business and advertisers first and foremost. There are probably several workable models that could be developed to achieve democratic media and communication, but until the issue is placed on the political agenda the discussion is undeveloped and hypothetical. One suspects that if a society like the United States devoted to this problem a mere fraction of the time it has devoted to commercializing communication, we could find some workable public service models.

With regard to journalism, the basic policy question to be addressed is how best to structure a media system to promote diversity of opinion, freedom of speech, and hard-hitting investigative journalism of the powers-that-be, all the while preventing any sector, especially the wealthy, from gaining undue influence. This is anything but a simple problem, for efforts to establish diversity may not encourage "watchdog" journalism and vice versa. But in the long run, all elements need to exist for each of them to prosper and for a democratic political culture to thrive.

This does not mean that there is no place for commercial media, merely that the *dominant* sector of the system must be nonprofit, noncommercial, and accountable to the public. Moreover, to the extent that commercial media and advertising play a role in a democratic media, they should be taxed to subsidize the nonprofit and noncommercial sector. A tax of, say, 1 percent on advertising would generate over $1.5 billion in 1997. Likewise, spectrum space should be leased (never auctioned) for commercial use, with the proceeds applied to support nonprofit and noncommercial media. Even at low estimates, rents on broadcast spectrum space could generate between 2 to 4 billion dollars annually. Combined, these monies could provide the basis for a viable, even extraordinary, noncommercial media culture. (For the sake of comparison, the *total* federal subsidy to public broadcasting in fiscal year 1997 is a mere $260 million, and it is to be reduced to $250 million in each of the subsequent two years.) Insofar as this noncommercial media sector would necessarily open up journalism and entertainment to themes and genres presently discouraged or ignored, it might also force the media giants to enrich and broaden their own fare.

Advertising should also be held to much higher standards for truth and accuracy than exist at present, and its insidious spread into every corner of our existence must be rolled back. (Aside from generating revenues for noncommercial media, a tax on advertising might also slow down the commercial tide.) Advertising must also be prevented from influencing media content. Europe provides examples of how to do this. Media ownership should be strictly regulated to prevent chains and conglomerates. Ben Bagdikian's notion that a media owner should be permitted to possess but one media outlet seems a commendable principle. It may be inefficient from a market perspective, but it is a small price to pay from a social perspective. It is worth noting that when the United States reorganized the Japanese media during its occupation following the Second World War, it placed limits on media ownership because it saw that concentrated media control could be a barrier to the formation of a political democracy.[73] It is time for the United States to take some of its own medicine.

In the immediate future, there are a few imperatives for media activists. We need to fight on behalf of public, community and public access broadcasting. This is far more than a battle among the elite for control of media turf. It is now more necessary than ever for public policy to mandate a well-funded, independent journalism, cultural and communication system. We need to roll back the movement to bring advertising to public broadcasting, and we need to make public broadcasting stations more accountable to the communities in which they are located. Once the principle of publicly funded broadcasting is abandoned, it will be ever more difficult to reinstate it. And once the principle is secure, we can pursue any number of creative measures to create a larger public sphere and to politicize our culture. We need to organize around estab-

ROBERT W. McCHESNEY

lishing public service standards for the Internet, to guarantee universal access and a healthy, preferably dominant, nonprofit and noncommercial sector. Independent of government policies, individuals and their nonprofit organizations need to pour resources into nonprofit and noncommercial media, for journalism and cultural fare. This involves radio, television, newspapers, magazines, video, and the Internet.

We also need to continue to critique the mainstream media and work to improve the quality of commercial journalism. Although the corporate media playing field is sloped heavily toward depoliticization and the concerns of the powerful, we need to do what it takes to assure the best possible journalism in that jaded context. It remains an important arena, as the right well understands.

The struggle for a democratic media system will be difficult. The opposition is wealthy, powerful and expert in ideological warfare. It effectively owns both major political parties. Its naked self-interest is draped in motherhood, the flag, the First Amendment, apple pie, and, of course, the mythological market; to hear their rhetoric, one would almost think the media, advertising and communications firms' existence divinely inspired. The corporate media also own most of the news media, so media activists arguably have an even more difficult time communicating with the public than other activists might face. But the cause is far from hopeless. In the past decade media activism has emerged from virtual non-existence to become a site of intense growth. Several media monitoring organizations have been formed, most notably Fairness & Accuracy In Reporting (FAIR), which has done a masterful job of educating the public and journalists to the nefarious influence on the media of corporate control, advertising, and the political right. In 1996 at least two new media activist groups were established: the Cultural Environment Movement and the less formal "Media and Democracy" group, based around a conference of the same name held in San Francisco. Both groups look to promote long-term structural change while working in broad coalitions and with grassroots community organizers.

Perhaps the central requirement for having a successful campaign for media reform will be to draw other progressive allies into the movement. In 1996 the media, computer and telecommunication industries were able to ram through the monstrous Telecommunications Act, to no small extent because the natural constituencies that should have been organizing against it were asleep at the switch. Likewise, the battle for nonprofit and noncommercial media will always be an uphill fight if public broadcasters are campaigning without organized support. The logical place to search for allies is among those sectors of the populace already cognizant of the need to maintain noncommercial public space and those sectors that realize the current corporate media system is hampering the nature of U.S. culture and democracy. In the former group are librarians and educators, among others. In the latter group are any variety of progressive social movements ranging from feminist, civil rights and environmental groups to many artists, religious organizations, and civil libertarians. Civil libertarians, in particular, must recognize that the market imposes a censorship every bit as insidi-

ROBERT W. McCHESNEY

ous as censorship by the state.

Regardless of what a progressive group's first issue of importance is, its second issue should be media and communication, because so long as the media are in corporate hands, the task of social change will be vastly more difficult, if not impossible, across the board. The biggest problem facing all who challenge the prerogatives of corporate rule is that the overwhelming majority of Americans are never exposed to anything remotely close to a reasoned, coherent, consistent, democratic socialist, pro-labor, or even old-fashioned New Deal Democratic perspective. This is why, in the end, media reform is inexorably intertwined with broader social and political reform. They rise or fall together. Any political party that claims to act on behalf of the bulk of the population, and against corporate rule, must incorporate progressive media and communications into the core of its platform. And, eventually, media reform will need to reach out to the broad sectors of society that are depoliticized or under the sway of rightist explanations (or other myths) of social decay. When the corporate, commercial basis of the media system is understood, media activists will find they have a potentially enormous base of support.

Two groups deserve particular attention. Organized labor has the single most important role to play, being uniquely situated with the resources and the perspective to battle the media and communication status quo. After a long hibernation, it is becoming understood among elements of the U.S. labor movement that labor's demise has been partially due to the right-wing ideological assault against unionism and progressive government policies, with which the commercial media have been effectively complicitous. In the 1940s there were approximately 1,000 full-time labor beat reporters and editors on U.S. daily newspapers. Today there are fewer than ten.[74] Labor needs to devote significant resources to the policy battles against profit-driven communication and for public broadcasting. It needs to subsidize a healthy, independent, noncommercial journalism and media. It needs to learn the conventions of mainstream journalism well enough to improve the amount and quality of its coverage. In sum, the labor movement needs to learn from its enemies and to take ideological warfare as seriously as economic warfare.

Specifically, journalist, entertainment and communication workers' trade unions are on the front lines of the struggle for democratic media. These unions need to recognize that traditional campaigns to protect jobs and benefits in the short term may enjoy some success, but they do nothing to address the long-term trajectory of their industries which is resolutely anti-labor. In Canada and parts of Europe, some similarly positioned unions are moving toward a position of providing a broader vision of communication in which workers and not investors are the representatives of the public interest. Communications unions are forming alliances with consumer and community groups, for example, to advocate a socially responsive vision of a non-market or at least well-regulated private telecommunication system. This is a model of progressive social unionism that may provide an escape route from the present downward spiral of U.S. communication unions, and is

ROBERT W. McCHESNEY

worthy of emulation by the labor movement as a whole.

The second important group for democratic media are the U.S. liberal and progressive foundations, which command large endowments for the promotion of social justice, civil rights, human welfare and democratic values. For years these foundations have eschewed involvement with media reform movements and with subsidizing nonprofit and noncommercial media, which they saw as outside their missions. At the same time, conservative foundations, which spend almost no money for social welfare, devote nearly the entirety of their resource base to ideological warfare against liberalism, labor and the left, with media activities being the central aspect of this work. Liberal and progressive foundations now find the social problems they are dedicated to addressing are growing worse due to the turn to the market and the dismantling of the welfare state, which in turn is due in part to the success of the pro-market ideological campaign bankrolled by conservative foundations. The liberal and progressive foundations need to recognize they are at an impasse. If they are serious about democracy, they are going to have to contribute to the establishment of the broad and rich media culture necessary for a democracy. They need to aggressively subsidize noncommercial and nonprofit media and journalism, as well as popular education campaigns concerning media ownership, control and policy-making. If they do not accept this challenge, the liberal and progressive foundations will be implicitly accepting the role of patching leaks on a sinking ship, instead of attempting to keep the leaks from forming.

Although the most important work is to be done at the local and national levels, this is also a global fight. The corporate media/communication system may well be the defining feature of the global market economy. This is true not only because of the rapidly growing economic, political and cultural roles of global commercial media, but also because communication technologies lay the basis for instantaneous global capital and currency markets. A main trend of global capitalism is that it undermines not only national sovereignty, but also popular sovereignty, as societies seem compelled to obey the dictates of global markets or face immediate and stern economic punishment. For the proponents of the market, like *Forbes* magazine, this is a welcome turn of events. It means that it is even less likely that "politics," i.e. the will of the people as citizens, can interfere with business's control over society.[75] It heralds a return to John Jay's famous maxim that "those who own the country ought to govern it."[76] Political debate, like democracy, will then be irrelevant.

Such a dark vision of our future should give us pause. In accepting (and encouraging) widening class divisions, the glorification of profit, greed and commercialism as the necessary cornerstones of our age, it portends grave damage to the human spirit and our ability to live together in viable communities. Our task is to push in the opposite direction, to create a public sphere and democratic media that can harness the creative vitality of our people and infuse it into our politics and culture. It is the push for genuine self-government. It is a necessary step toward building a fair, humane, and sustainable society.

ENDNOTES

[1] Quotation from Edward S. Herman, *Beyond Hypocrisy* (Boston: South End Press, 1992), p. 2.

[2] Jurgen Habermas, *The Structural Transformation of the Public Sphere*, Thomas Burger with Frederick Lawrence, translators (Cambridge, Mass.: MIT Press, 1989). Originally published in German in 1962.

[3] Cited in Frank Luther Mott, *American Journalism* (New York: The Macmillan Company, 1941), p. 405.

[4] See Gerald J. Baldasty, *The Commercialization of the News* (Madison: University of Wisconsin Press, 1992).

[5] Ben H. Bagdikian, *The Media Monopoly*, fourth edition (Boston: Beacon Press, 1992).

[6] See Alex Carey, *Taking the Risk Out of Democracy* (Champaign: University of Illinois Press, 1996).

[7] See C. Wright Mills, *The Power Elite* (New York: Oxford University Press, 1956).

[8] See C. B. Macpherson, *The Life and Times of Liberal Democracy* (New York: Oxford University Press, 1977).

[9] Milton Friedman, *Capitalism and Freedom* (Chicago: University of Chicago Press, 1962), ch. 2; see also, David Kelley and Roger Downey, "Liberalism and Free Speech," in Judith Lichtenberg, editor, Democracy and the Mass Media (Cambridge and New York: Cambridge University Press, 1990), pp. 66-101.

[10] See Noam Chomsky, *On Power and Ideology: The Managua Lectures* (Boston: South End Press, 1987).

[11] See Gaye Tuchman, *Making News* (New York: Basic Books, 1978); Mark Fishman, *Manufacturing the News* (Austin: University of Texas Press, 1980); Herbert Gans, *Deciding What's News* (New York: Pantheon, 1979).

[12] Edward S. Herman and Noam Chomsky, *Manufacturing Consent: The Political Economy of the Mass Media* (New York: Pantheon, 1988).

[13] See W. Lance Bennett, News: *The Politics of Illusion* (New York: Longman, 1983); Robert Entman, *Democracy Without Citizens* (New York: Oxford University Press, 1989); Michael Morgan, Justin Lewis and Sut Jhally, "More Viewing, Less Knowing," in Hamid Mowlana, George Gerbner and Herbert I. Schiller, editors, Triumph of the Image (Boulder, Col.: Westview Press, 1992).

14 Diane Mermigas, "Still to come: smaller media alliances," *Electronic Media*, February 5, 1996, p. 38.

15 Doug Wilson, *Strategies of the Media Giants* (London: Pearson Professional Ltd., 1996), p. 5.

16 See Edward S. Herman and Robert W. McChesney, *The Global Media: The New Missionaries of Global Capitalism* (London: Cassell, 1997).

17 Marla Matzer, "Contented Kingdoms," *Superbrands '97*, supplement to *Adweek*, October 7, 1996, pp. 30, 33.

18 Bernard Simon, "Seagram to hold on to 15% stake in Time Warner," *The Financial Times*, June 1, 1995, p. 18.

19 Raymond Snoddy, "Master of bits at home in the hub," *Financial Times*, May 28, 1996, p. 17.

20 Catherine E. Celebrezze, "The Man Who Bought the Media," *Extra!*, Vol. 9, No. 2, March-April 1996, pp. 21-22.

21 Ronald Grover, "Plenty of Dreams, Not Enough Work?" *Business Week*, July 22, 1996, p. 65.

22 Paula Dwyer, "Can Rupert Conquer Europe?" *Business Week*, March 25, 1996, p. 169.

23 Raymond Snoddy, "Master of bits at home in the hub," *Financial Times*, May 28, 1996, p. 17.

24 Elizabeth Jensen and Eben Shapiro, "Time Warner's Fight With News Corp. Belies Mutual dependence," *The Wall Street Journal*, October 28, 1996, p. A1.

25 Alison Carper, "Paint-By-Numbers Journalism: How Reader Surveys and Focus Groups Subvert a Democratic Press," Discussion paper D-19, Joan Shorenstein Center on the Press, Politics and Public Policy, April 1995.

26 Dorothy Rabinowitz, "Cronkite Returns to Airwaves," *The Wall Street Journal*, December 9, 1996, p. A12.

27 Penn Kimball, *Downsizing the News: Network Cutbacks in the Nation's Capital* (Washington, D.C.: Woodrow Wilson Center Press, 1994).

28 See, for example, Mort Rosenblum, *Who Stole the News?* (New York: John Wiley & Sons, 1993); Doug Underwood, *When MBAs Rule the Newsroom: How the Marketers and Managers are Reshaping Today's Media* (New York: Columbia University Press, 1993); John McManus, *Market-Driven Journalism: Let the Citizen Beware!* (Thousand Oaks, Cal.: Sage, 1994); Dennis Mazzocco, *Networks of Power: Corporate TV's Threat to Democracy* (Boston: South End Press, 1994).

ROBERT W. McCHESNEY

[29] James Squires, *Read All About It! The Corporate Takeover of America's Newspapers* (New York: Times Books, 1993).

[30] Elizabeth Lesly, "Self-Censorship Is Still Censorship," *Business Week*, December 16, 1996, p. 78.

[31] See John Stauber and Sheldon Rampton, *Toxic Sludge is Good for You: Lies, Damn Lies and the Public Relations Industry* (Monroe, Maine: Common Courage Press, 1995).

[32] Institute for Alternative Journalism, "Media and Democracy: a blueprint for reinvigorating public life in the Information Age," working paper, December 1996, p. 4.

[33] Andre Schiffrin, "The Corporatization of Publishing," *The Nation*, June 3, 1996, pp. 29-32.

[34] Leonard Klady, "Why mega-flicks click," *Variety*, November 25-December 1, 1996, p. 1.

[35] Barbara Maltsby, "The Homogenization of Hollywood," *Media Studies Journal*, 10 (2-3) (Spring/Summer 1996): p. 115.

[36] Bill Carter, "Pow! Thwack! Bam! No Dubbing Needed," *The New York Times*, Week in Review section, November 3, 1996, p. 6.

[37] Bruce Orwall, "Disney Chases Live-Action Merchandising Hits," *The Wall Street Journal*, November 27, 1996, p. B1

[38] Luisa Kroll, "Entertainomercials," *Forbes*, November 4, 1996, p. 322, 324.

[39] Mary Kuntz and Joseph Weber, "The New Hucksterism," *Business Week*, July 1, 1996, pp. 77-84.

[40] Michael Schneider, "Brand name-dropping," *Electronic Media*, August 26, 1996, pp. 1, 30.

[41] Mary Kuntz and Joseph Weber, "The New Hucksterism," *Business Week*, July 1, 1996, pp. 77-84.

[42] Mary Kuntz and Joseph Weber, "The New Hucksterism," *Business Week*, July 1, 1996, p. 82.

[43] Sally Goll Beatty, "CNBC Will Air A Show Owned, Vetted by IBM," *The Wall Street Journal*, June 4, 1996, pp. B1, B8.

[44] Raymond Snoddy and Alan Cane, "Full multimedia impact years away, says Murdoch," *Financial Times*, May 12, 1995, p. 1.

[45] Brent Schlender, "A Conversation with the Lords of Wintel," *Fortune*, July 8, 1996, p. 46.

[46] David Lieberman, "Old guard tactic is old brand names," *USA Today*, International Edition, July 19, 1996, p. 8A.

47 Tony Jackson, "MCI sees the future in 'one-stop' services," *Financial Times*, August 8, 1996, p. 15.

48 "Global Telecom Alliances," *Information Week*, November 13, 1995, p. 40; Michael Lindemann, "Telecoms operators launch global alliance,' *Financial Times*, February 1, 1996, p. 16.

49 "The world of giant telecoms," *Financial Times*, April 2, 1996, p. 13.

50 John J. Keller and Gautam Nauk, "PacTel-SBC Merger Is Likely to Ring In An Era of Alliances Among Baby Bells," *The Wall Street Journal*, April 2, 1996, p. B1.

51 Danielle Robinson, "Opening up the markets in US telecoms," *The Independent*, February 13, 1996, p. 24.

52 Don Clark, "Microsoft's On-Line Service Goes to a TV format," *The Wall Street Journal*, December 9, 1996, p. B8.

53 Michael Krantz, "The Webmeister of AT&T," *Mediaweek*, November 20, 1995, p. 17.

54 Frank Beacham, "Net Loss," *Extra!*, May-June 1996, p. 16.

55 This story is told in greater detail in Robert W. McChesney, *Telecommunications, Mass Media, and Democracy: The Battle for the Control of U.S. Broadcasting, 1928-1935* (New York: Oxford University Press, 1993).

56 Charles Bien to author, July 6, 1995.

57 Quotation from Jeff Cohen and Norman Solomon, *Through the Media Looking Glass* (Monroe, Maine: Common Courage Press, 1995), p. 258.

58 Addrienne Ward Fawcett, "Interactive awareness growing," *Advertising Age*, October 16, 1996, p. 20.

59 William Leiss, Stephen Kline and Sut Jhally, *Social Communication in Advertising*, second edition (Scarborough, Ontario: Nelson Canada), ch. 10.

60 Norman Solomon, "Hucksters are milking a Sacred Media Cow," syndicated newspaper column, November 23, 1996.

61 See, for example, Paul M. Barrett, "Supreme Court Makes It Harder to Limit Ads," *The Wall Street Journal*, May 14, 1996, p. B1.

62 Molly Ivins, "New populism says America is ours, and we want it back," *The Capital Times*, December 2, 1996, p. 1C.

63 See Herbert I. Schiller, *Culture, Inc.* (New York: Oxford University Press, 1989).

[64] I thank Scott Sherman for providing me this quotation from the French newspaper *Combat*.

[65] Mary Vipond, *Listening In: The First Decade of Canadian Broadcasting, 1922-1932* (Montreal and Kingston: McGill University Press, 1992).

[66] Joel Brinkley, "Defining TV's and Computers For a Future of High Definition," *The New York Times*, December 2, 1996, p. C1.

[67] See, for example, L. Brent Bozell III and Brent H. Baker, *And That's The Way It Isn't* (Alexandria, Virginia: Media Research Center, 1990); William A. Rusher, *The Coming Battle for the Media* (New York: William Morrow and Company, 1988); S. Robert Lichter, Stanley Rothman, and Linda S. Lichter, *The Media Elite* (Bethesda, Md.: Adler & Adler, 1986).

[68] Jeff Gerth, "Business gains With Democrats," *The New York Times*, December 25, 1996, p. A11.

[69] Robert Parry, "Lost History: Rise of the Right-Wing Machine," *The Consortium*, November 25, 1996, pp. 3-5.

[70] See Michael Medved, *Hollywood Vs. America: Popular Culture and the War on Traditional Culture* (New York: HarperCollins, 1992). For a more subtle version of the argument, see S. Robert Lichter, Linda S. Lichter and Stanley Rothman, *Watching America* (New York: Prentice Hall Press, 1991).

[71] See Kathryn S. Olmstead, Challenging the Secret Government (Chapel Hill: The University of North Carolina Press, 1996).

[72] *Extra!*, March-April 1995, p. 2. I thank Jeff Cohen for the Helms quote.

[73] D. Eleanor Westney, "Mass Media as Business Organizations: A U.S. Japanese Comparison," in Susan Pharr and Ellis Krauss, editors, *Media and Politics in Japan* (Honolulu: University of Hawaii Press, 1996), pp. 54-56.

[74] See, for example, William J. Puette, *Through Jaundiced Eyes: How the Media View Organized Labor* (Ithaca, N.Y.: ILR Press, 1992).

[75] Peter Huber, "Cyberpower," *Forbes*, December 2, 1996, pp. 142-147.

[76] Quotation in Noam Chomsky, *Keeping the Rabble in Line: Interviews with David Barsamian* (Monroe, Maine: Common Courage Press, 1994), p. 247.

ROBERT W. McCHESNEY is Associate Professor in the School of Journalism and Mass Communication at the University of Wisconsin-Madison. He thanks Vivek Chibber, Edward S. Herman, John Nerone, Dan Schiller, John Bellamy "Duke" Foster, Jeff Cohen, Paul Hass, John Nichols, Inger Stole, Norman Solomon, David Barsamian, and George Gerbner for their comments on earlier drafts.